Animals in my Backyard
OPOSSUMS

Jordan McGill

www.av2books.com

Go to **www.av2books.com**, and enter this book's unique code.

BOOK CODE

X835470

AV² by Weigl brings you media enhanced books that support active learning.

AV² provides enriched content that supplements and complements this book. Weigl's AV² books strive to create inspired learning and engage young minds in a total learning experience.

Your AV² Media Enhanced books come alive with...

 Audio
Listen to sections of the book read aloud.

 **Video**
Watch informative video clips.

Embedded Weblinks
Gain additional information for research.

Try This!
Complete activities and hands-on experiments.

 Key Words
Study vocabulary, and complete a matching word activity.

 Quizzes
Test your knowledge.

 Slide Show
View images and captions, and prepare a presentation.

... and much, much more!

Published by AV² by Weigl
350 5th Avenue, 59th Floor New York, NY 10118
Website: www.av2books.com www.weigl.com

Library of Congress Cataloging-in-Publication Data

McGill, Jordan.
 Opossums / Jordan McGill.
   p. cm. -- (Animals in my backyard)
 ISBN 978-1-61690-933-8 (hardcover : alk. paper) -- ISBN 978-1-61690-579-8 (online)
 1. Opossums--Juvenile literature. I. Title.
 QL737.M34M44 2012
 599.2'76--dc23
                        2011023421

062011
WEP030611

Project Coordinator: Jordan McGill Art Director: Terry Paulhus

Weigl acknowledges Getty Images as the primary image supplier for this title.

Catherine L. Sherman; page 12

Animals in my Backyard
OPOSSUMS

CONTENTS

Meet the opossum.

She is about the size of a pet cat.

She cares for her babies
and puts them in her pouch.

In her pouch, her babies eat
and grow.

7

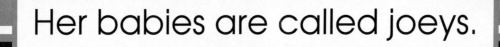
Her babies are called joeys.

Joeys ride on her back.

She smells with her nose.

With her nose,
she can find food.

She eats almost any foods she finds.

Foods she finds are insects, fruits, grasses, and eggs.

She climbs high up in trees.

High up in trees, she moves around with help from her tail.

She eats with 50 sharp teeth.

With 50 sharp teeth,
she scares off other animals.

She likes to be up high,
but she lives below the ground.

Below the ground,
she makes a home with leaves.

If you meet the opossum,
she might play dead.
Do not touch her.

If you meet the opossum,
stay away.

OPOSSUM FACTS

This page provides more detail about the interesting facts found in the book.
Simply look for the corresponding page number to match the fact.

Pages 4-5

Opossums are the size of a large house cat. Their pointed faces are white with a pink nose. They have hairless black ears. Opossums can be 7 to 41 inches (17 to 104 centimeters) long, including their tail. An opossum is a type of mammal called a marsupial. Marsupials live in their mother's pouch when they are young.

Pages 6–7

An opossum baby is called a joey. A joey is about the size of a honeybee at birth. Once born, joeys live in their mother's pouch for two months. In the pouch, they feed on their mother's milk and begin to grow. Without their mother's pouch, they would not be able to survive into adulthood.

Pages 8–9

After a few months, the babies will peek out of their mother's pouch for the first time. After they leave the pouch, they continue to grow. When they are young, they often return to their mother's pouch and ride on her back. By about one year of age, an opossum is full grown and ready to go off on its own.

Pages 10–11

Opossums have a keen sense of smell. They use their sense of smell to search for food. Opossums do not see or hear well, so they also use their sense of smell to navigate their environment and avoid danger.

Opossums are omnivores. This means they eat both plants and animals. A main part of their diet is insects. They eat crickets, beetles, butterflies, worms, and grubs. In spring, opossums feed on bird eggs. Frogs, lizards, snakes, and small rabbits also are part of their diet. Opossums eat a large variety of fruit and berries.

An opossums' feet and long tail are suited for climbing trees. They climb trees to escape predators. The opossum has five toes, with claws on each of its front feet. Each hind foot has four clawed toes and an opposable thumb. This, along with its strong tail, allows the opossum to climb with ease.

Opossums have 50 teeth in their mouth. They have more teeth than any other land mammal in North America. The teeth help them chew. Opossums show their teeth to scare away enemies. Opossums hiss or screech if they feel threatened.

Opossums live in forests near streams across North America. They can be found high up in trees or in hollow logs along the ground. Some live in abandoned, or empty, groundhog holes. Opossums' homes are called dens. They make nests of leaves in their dens.

Sometimes, an opossum pretends to be dead if it is scared. It rolls over, shuts its eyes, and sticks out its tongue. The opossum can lie still for hours. Most often, an opossum will run away when scared. If a person encounters an opossum, whether it is laying still or on the move, he or she should stay back. An opossum will bite, and if it is playing dead, it is afraid.

WORD LIST

Research has shown that as much as 65 percent of all written material published in English is made up of 300 words. These 300 words cannot be taught using pictures or learned by sounding them out. They must be recognized by sight. This book contains 51 common sight words to help young readers improve their reading fluency and comprehension. This book also teaches young readers several important content words. These words are paired with pictures to aid in learning and improve understanding.

Page	Sight Words First Appearance	Page	Content Words First Appearance
4	the	4	opossum
5	a, about, is, of, she	5	cat, pet, size
6	and, eat, for, grow, her, in, puts, them	6	babies, pouch
8	are, called	8	joeys
9	back, on	10	nose
10	with	13	eggs, fruits, grasses, insects
11	can, find, food	15	tail
12	almost, any, eats	16	teeth
14	high, trees, up, walks	18	ground
15	around, from, help, moves	19	leaves
16	animals, off, other		
18	be, below, but, likes, lives, to		
19	home, makes		
21	away, do, if, might, not, play, you		

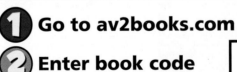